IRUM IBRAHIM

NOTHING
TO
SUMMIT

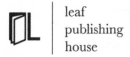

leaf
publishing
house

Dedicated to my late grandfather, who saw a skill in me before anyone else, and continuously encouraged me to write more.

CONTENTS

CHAPTER ONE: PREPARATION

The wind outside was making the windows shake; the weather was signaling to Zohra that a thunderstorm was coming. She swept aside her thick, green embroidered bedroom curtains and peeked outside. A dark blue hue filled the sky along with light gray-colored cumulus clouds. Slightly troubled, she made an effort to ignore the weather and continued to gather all she needed for her climb the next morning. The determined 18-year-old was setting off to climb the Hyalite Peak in Montana, on her own.

She lay out her orange Evolv climbing shoes next to her bedroom door and folded an extra pair of underwear, socks, and undershirt into her big, bulky backpack, along with a 1-liter water bottle, a prayer rug, compass, sunscreen, sunglasses and dry food for the day. She also set aside a soft shell pant, insulated jacket, waterproof jacket, pants, and gloves. Then she pulled out her brand new notebook that she had been saving for this journey.

"Finally — a new journal," she said, exhaling. "A new beginning. I can't wait to see what this climb will be like and where it will take me."

She dated the blank page "January 1, 2012" in the top right-hand corner, and then wrote the exact words she had just said aloud with a black pen. She continued to write.

"I'm nervous but so excited at the same time. I'm unsure of what's to come and whether or not I'll make it to the top. However, I want to prove my doubts wrong. Also, when I think that way, I'm reminded that all and any obstacles that tread my path will help me, not hurt me, because they are given by God. They're blessings in disguise."

Zohra put down her pen and stared at her words. She was exhausted because of these fears of failure clouding her thoughts.

"I'm going to wash my face, brush my teeth, and go to sleep," she said to herself. "I need to wake up early, pray Fajr, eat a good breakfast, hydrate myself and be mentally prepared for this. I can't let my fears consume me."

And then she repeated that last sentence over and over until she fell asleep.

THE MOUNTAIN

We all have a million and one dreams.

There are always a million and one ways to reach those dreams.

You look up at this massive mountain towering over you, thinking you'll never be able to reach the top. You feel overwhelmed with its vastness, knowing there are so many paths you can take to reach your destination.

However, you can't move. You're too afraid of the struggle, and those fears seem to escalate because they're rooted from false notions — pure ignorance. You haven't opened your eyes to the bigger picture yet.

The path and the destination go together. You can't focus too much on either, because if your dream doesn't take you closer to Him, then where are you going?

You will fail to notice the trees around you whose roots, branches, and bark hold so much wisdom. You fail to see the way the stream makes each rock and pebble within shine so brilliantly. You fail to notice the vastness of the sky and how it provides the perfect backdrop to any image, every single time. By overlooking the path because you are focused on the destination, you do not notice any of these things. Lack of focus may cause the target to become yet another task to work towards instead of a trip that is there for your taking.

What's so special about the top of the mountain?

Analyze.

What makes you dream this dream? Keep asking your heart questions and use your mind to find solutions, but don't let the logic of your mind silence your heart. Trust your heart, listen to it, feel it; your heart is your biggest ally. You have to dig deeper, so you can find Him there. When you see Him, you'll learn to listen to the voice of your heart and mind. You'll start getting accustomed to the sound, finding harmony between their friction.

Trying to reach the top doesn't mean you're achieving your dream. Your dreams are the path that take you to the top — your final destination to Him. You can't make your thoughts your goal; you have to make your thoughts help you reach your goal.

Everything you work for should help you create right in this world, for the Next world. When you write, aim to release your frustration, pain, and sadness while hoping to help open eyes. When you study, remember that your hard work, patience, and struggle will not attain reward with an A+, but His pleasure. When you love someone, love them for His sake, and praise the Creator for placing that indescribable feeling in your heart.

Your dreams should act as a bridge between you and God. If you're having trouble walking, know that you need to do a double take on your goals. Let them be a means to reach your ends. Not merely a worldly desire.

So when you stand below this mountain, tell yourself that your journey is eternal. Your dreams will help you get there, as long as you walk with purified intentions and His name in your heart. His light will guide you to your destination, and help you endure the struggle with open eyes. His words will recharge you, and His remembrance will be the water that quenches your thirst. Don't be so afraid. Know that He's got you.

Bismillah.

PLANTING THE SEED

"Not equal are the evil and the good, although the abundance of evil might impress you. So, fear Allah, oh you of understanding, so that you may be successful." - (The Qur'an, 5:100)

While there are two Arabic words used for "successful," it's interesting to see which one Allah (SWT) used in this particular verse.

He didn't say *"la 'allakum tafuzoon."* *Tafuzoon* translates to success concerning winning, but winning something that's short term. Instead, He uses the word *tuflihun*, which translates to achieving success through hard work. Its root word, *iflah*, is used when you farm or tend to your crops. It's used when you plant a seed, nourish the soil with water, and make sure it gets enough sun — preventing weeds from spreading. You work hard on your crops all year long and then eventually, whether it is before or after failure, you see success.

The Qur'an is so perfect. Every single word, verse, and chapter has depth and meaning so deeply intertwined within it — it would take us more than a lifetime to fully grasp the extent of His Book's profundity.

In this single verse, our Creator tells us how to achieve our ultimate goal of success in this world and the Next. He tells us that looking for the good in a world that's absorbed in filth is going to be hard work, but the reward of success will come with it. The results of your labor will surface with time: be patient and persistent. In the end, our *sabr*, or patience, in light of loss is what God is testing, through these circumstances that we deem "unfortunate" so very often.

THE GREATEST SHIELD

When you're living in a world that forces you to defeat a particular enemy on a daily basis, life isn't quite so ordinary.

There are always questions to be asked (and answered), plots to be made, plans to be created, all in light of weakening and ultimately defeating that one enemy of yours, right? You try to figure out his ways. You search everywhere for some hidden clues to perhaps help you in your fight against *Shaytan*, the accursed whisperer.

Every single day is a fight against the whisperer. Every single day, you try to diffuse his whispers, weaken his strength, and build your own in the midst of it all. How? You pray five times a day, give charity, and fast during *Ramadan*. You work on the pillars of your home.

Sometimes, though, all of that is not enough. Your sincerity and your fear of God is lacking, and you don't know why. So, you ask Him for His guidance and mercy as a desperate slave who's strayed from his Master and become a slave of his *nafs* (ego), instead. You've put yourself in such a mess, and now, the only way out is through your search for the straight path. You ask Him to open your eyes and your heart, not just to reflect, but to act by what you learned while reflecting.

This is how we strengthen ourselves. Sometimes He, being the Most Merciful, inherently weakens the *Shaytan* in the most simple yet profound of ways, like when we make the call for prayer, or simply recite the words *a'udhu billahi min ash-shaytaan-i'r rajeem* (I seek refuge in Allah from the accursed Satan). His help doesn't stop there, though. Of course not. God even quotes the *Shaytan* in His Book, to let us know what his inner workings are. He tells us all about his sly techniques, tendencies, likes and dislikes.

The *Shaytan* was talking to God privately, telling him how he intends to misguide us.

"Because You have put me in error, I will surely sit in wait for them on Your straight path. Then I will come to them from before them and from behind them and on their right, and their left, and You will not find most of them grateful [to You]." - (The Qur'an, 7:16-17)

Look at the profound wisdom behind this. God wanted us to know what mechanism the whisperer will use so that we can ultimately repel his whispers.

After God rejects the *Shaytan* and removes him from the presence of Allah, the *Shaytan* responds: "Then I will come to them from before them and from behind them and on their right..."

"... and You will not find most of them grateful [to You]."

This is how the whisperer intends to distance a person from Allah. The moment you find yourself being ungrateful and complaining, you know you've lost. And no, not just the battle against the *Shaytan*, you've failed in learning your lesson of thankfulness. The two go together.

Be continuously grateful. Avoid complaining. Be patient. Find the extremes of benefit in what you deem a misfortune. If you look at the most important relationships you have in life (with Allah, the Prophet (SAW), your parents, and your spouse) you'll always find complaints, and when those complaints aren't controlled, they lead to much greater disconnects. Rather than being grateful to God that He's blessed us with a halal marriage, we complain to our spouses about trivial matters that only escalate with time. The complaining itself becomes incessant and regressive. Stop. Thank each other. Find the good, and God will increase your marriage in peace. We all marry a deficient human being. The purpose of your bond is to find the good in each other and subsequently be blessed with peace, through His pleasure and love.

It all begins with an ungratefulness for Allah (SWT)'s decree and builds from there. You can't just thank Him, you have to thank everyone for what they do for you and bring it back to Him in the end.

Thank people who come from every direction, because the *Shaytan* comes from all around you. Look at your present state and thank Him for all your blessings — with a promise to work on living a better life here to get There, in a way that's pleasurable to Him. Look at the people around you and be grateful for their presence and company. Our Prophet (SAW) was always incredibly thankful for his companions.

THE WAIT

There's a pain in not knowing what's to come. There's strength in making consistent *du'a* (invocation). And there's faith in trusting His will.

Destiny is a funny thing. You have to work towards what you're trying to achieve or receive, yet God already knows what's to come for you. That's your test — how hard will you work toward your goal? How consistent will you be with your *du'a?* Will you let the *Shaytan* win the battle, and lose all hope in the height of His throne?

Don't. Endure that pain. Why do you keep numbing it with your bad habits? You're doing it all wrong. You're so impatient. Wait. Find your path into the unknown world of patience.

This pain and sadness will only help you. It'll help you grow and increase the strength within.

Don't lose hope in the troubles you're faced with. This world was made to plant seeds of pain within and all around us. The ultimate test is how we decide to nurture those seeds.

God wants to test your patience. Don't give up now.

CHAPTER TWO: CLIMB

The dawn (Fajr) prayer alarm went off at 5:30 a.m. and the sound of it made Zohra want to throw her phone against the wall. Reminding herself that she needs to get up to pray, she calmed herself down, put her alarm on snooze, and then slowly got herself out of bed about 5 minutes later.

Yawning, Zohra extended her arm to pick up the glass of water on her bedside table. After taking a few sips, she headed to the bathroom sink and stood in front of the mirror, staring at herself for about 30 seconds.

Her eyes were filled with fear and hope.

"AHHH. I hope I can do this," she whispered.

She turned on the faucet, and cold water began running through her hands. She splashed it on her face and continued to complete the remaining steps of wudhu (ablution for prayer).

As Zohra stood on top of the prayer mat, she grabbed her bluish-gray colored scarf from her bed and quickly wrapped it around her head.

"Allah Hu-Akbar (God is the Greatest)," she began.

After praying and making du'a — she quietly walked into her sister's room to wake her up.

"Jiyaaaa," she said softly.

Then she raised her voice a bit.

"Jiyaaaa, come on, you have to drop me off," she said, as she shook her sister's shoulder.

Jiya rubbed her eyes and said, "Okay, go, I'm about to get ready. I'll be done in like 15 minutes."

Zohra knew what that meant. Her sister was going to take 45 minutes minimum, so she pulled out her notebook and began writing.

"Today is finally the big day. I've been training for this climb for years now, and although I've been determined throughout, I'm

starting to get cold feet. NOW. Right before I have to head out. Also, it's because I KNOW it won't be easy and there will be obstacles, but I'm just afraid to face them. "

Zohra continued, and about 40 minutes later, she heard her name being called.

"Come on!" Jiya yelled from downstairs. "I'm warming up the car, hurry up."

"Okay!" Zohra yelled back. "I'm coming. Wait."

"I'm trying to teach myself patience in these few hours of turbulence before the climb. I used to think that patience is all about waiting for the storm to pass. However, it's actually about understanding that storms don't just pass and never come back again. They will always come back. So you have to be patient enough to understand how to stand in the middle of the storm, in peace, smiling. You have to be grateful for the rain and appreciate the thunder," she wrote, finishing up her thought.

Quickly skipping down the stairs, Zohra held tight to her notebook and then found her shoes. She held her journal in her left hand as she put on her boots with her right. Then, she double-checked her bag to make sure she had everything she needed, gave her home one last look, and then stepped outside, shutting the door behind her.

Hopping in the car and taking a deep breath, Zohra softly whispered, "Bismillah."

"Are you sure you're ready for this?" Jiya asked her sister.

"I've been preparing for years now. I'll never feel ready, but I think that's how I know that I am. I know that of course, this journey won't be perfect, but that's why I need to pursue it. I want to learn how to face the obstacles."

"If that's how you feel, then I fully support you," Jiya replied with confidence. "And honestly, I'm proud of you for being so determined."

The two drove for another 30 minutes until they reached the mountain stop for climbers. Jiya got out of the car and gave Zohra the tightest hug.

"I love you," she said.

They parted ways. Zohra tugged on each strap of her backpack on each side of her upper arm, as she looked up at the mountain in wonder.

"WOW," she exclaimed. "Bismillah."

She walked up to the mountain and took the first step. She eased into the climb quickly, and her anxiety began to dissipate.

In the far distance, she saw another girl climbing up.

"Wow, there's someone else here?" she asked herself. "I need to catch up to her."

Zohra knew it would be helpful to know someone else climbing, although she intended to climb this mountain as a solo journey.

She didn't speed up, in any case. She told herself that if she's meant to meet the other climber, she will, but she maintained her speed for a better chance.

About an hour later, Zohra found herself very close to the other climber. The lady was tall with a stronger build than Zohra. She had beautiful, dark brown skin and dark hair that was tied up in a bun, with a few strands on each side of her face.

Now, Zohra sped up just a bit until she got to the older lady who must have been in her late twenties.

"Hi!" Zohra exclaimed. "I'm so glad you're here! I thought I was completely alone on this journey, and even though that's what I intended, I was starting to feel slightly lost."

"Hey! Wow. What a pleasant surprise for myself as well."

The lady held out her hand to shake with Zohra and said, "My name is Tahira. Yours?"

Zohra shared her name and background, and was pleasantly surprised to learn that Tahira climbed this mountain once each week. They both took a break from the climb, drank water, re-energized themselves, and chatted for almost 45 minutes. It was almost scary how similar they were to one another. Tahira was nearly eight years older than Zohra, but she was the wiser, more experienced one. Zohra felt like she was speaking to an older version of herself, or at least, a version of herself that she aspired to be like.

So far, the climb had been smoother than Zohra thought it would be. She found an excellent companion and wasn't too tired or exhausted yet. She found a good pace of climbing and wanted to take her time, maintaining her speed.

MISGUIDED

I hate thinking my efforts are going to waste.

It's hard not to let that thought come across your mind though, and it's even harder not to let it make you want to give up, and forget both your initial and ultimate purpose.

Even when you think you've wasted time, you have to remember that God never wastes your time. You can extract lessons from every single situation if you ponder rather than glance, using your heart instead of your eyes. When you feel like you haven't been rewarded for what you've worked for, take advantage of that moment to humble yourself. Reflect. Maybe He wants you to work harder. Perhaps He's testing your strength.

And maybe, you'll never even find recompense in this world.

Once you control the desire to visibly see your reward in this world and channel it into a pure passion, your intentions will shift.

When you're always searching for a prize, you're losing track of your purpose. Remember, you're not doing this to gain love or respect from the people around you. Any connection you're given in this world comes from God alone. That doesn't mean to *just* start with *Bismillah* and end with *Alhamdulilah*. The entirety of your words, thoughts, and actions should always take you back to their Source. Only then can you put your absolute trust in His decree, with a clear mind and pure heart. Only then can you honestly feel indifferent about the respect others are or aren't giving you. You know you're working, giving, and loving, ultimately for Him alone.

Live in the essence of His love and mercy to understand the in-depth lessons within your misguided efforts. Keep purifying your intentions. Keep failing, falling, and getting back up.

TRY

Every sin gives the believing sinner pain. However, sometimes the pain hits you with so much force that you tell yourself you've finally reached the limit. You've entered a halt. It's like you've finally fallen so hard, that you know for sure you'll walk with more caution next time.

But then you fall again. Your arrogance failed you, yet again. You wished for self-assurance without even thinking about Allah's assurance. That's the most flawed logic I've ever heard of.

Man.

Each time you sin, you learn a different lesson and discover a new kind of pain. It's a vicious cycle. Human beings were made to sin and repent. You can't ever get out of the cycle completely, but you can keep trying, and eventually slow it down until it's almost stagnant. But even before that, you have to focus on re-organizing your goals. Your primary aim shouldn't be to stop sinning, but to first understand and learn from those falls. Your attempt to break a bad habit without proper knowledge of its consequences will only lead to incessant holes, while you journey to fight *Shaytan*.

You can extract lessons from every single situation you encounter. Keep your eyes open while you're falling, so you can learn from the internal pain before the external, instead of letting it subside completely. Remind yourself of God, even if you're committing the gravest of sins. You'll hear *Shaytan's* whispers telling you to give up, and that you'll never get to where you want to be regarding your *imaan*, or faith. Fight those whispers. All the *Shaytan* wants for you is to give in to them instead, and lose sight of your already receding will to surrender and submit to Him alone.

The whisperer is your enemy; you have to thoroughly learn his tricks and techniques to defeat him. His purpose, ultimate goal, and aim are to never tire from making you stray from the straight path. Your mission, ultimate goal, and objectives are to never tire from fighting off his every whisper and repenting to your Lord with utmost sincerity.

Never think you've reached a halt when it comes to sin. That kind of thinking is a form of great arrogance, and very different from an intention to not sin again. You're a human, not an angel. Don't think of yourself as one — you'll fall and fail, and will have to get back up again. You don't have control over that. All you have control over is whether you choose to use your falls and failures to your advantage. How do you decide to stand back up again? With a firmer grip on God's rope, or a weaker one?

No matter what the case may be, don't let yourself get discouraged by your sinning or the pain it triggers, to the point where you give up. You have to keep trying harder and harder. Peace lies in struggling for the sake of God's pleasure, even if you can't find it initially.

The storms will come, over and over. You'll hear the whispers all the time. But with every test you pass, the vicious cycle will slow down. All you have to do is keep your eyes open, fearing nothing but Him alone. Try your hardest to succeed, but be prepared for failure. It's inevitable, and the only way to ever succeed later on. Don't be afraid of the pain and lessons. They're just trees of knowledge.

KILLING FEAR WITH FEAR

We all know that the only way to stop worrying about the future of our success is to remember that our time here is limited. We all know that our last day here is uncertain. We know, but that's what the problem is, it's that we *just* know.

Knowledge may make you feel liberated, but it won't liberate you unless you apply it to your life. You have to increase the fear of God in your heart. A fear that coincides with your love. A fear that allows you to live in peace here, knowing that the quality of your sincerity, intention, and effort is what will dictate your place There. A fear so strong that it overcomes every other fear inside you.

When you know you lack *taqwa* — the fear of God — you have to put extra effort into building that shield around yourself, to guard you against all that angers Him, whether it's a word, a thought, or an action. This is you making a mental effort to act in accordance to God's law. And He'll help you out as long as you're persistent and sincere in your *du'a* (invocation) to be granted guidance. Ask Him to give you strength, to increase your *taqwa*, to submit to Him entirely, and to live in surrender to His word. Don't worry about how far-fetched your *du'a* sounds. He knows what's in your heart. And no matter where you are in your journey toward becoming a more devout Muslim, the sincerity in your desire to reach those goals will give you the ability to reach them. Once you have that down, focus on your intention.

You're working in the present moment for the Hereafter, knowing that you'll fall multiple times. Don't get discouraged by those falls at all — they're blessings in disguise that you need to extract lessons from, to keep you moving forward. You'll think you can't take the pain and the obstacles that He blesses you with, but you'll fall seven times and stand up eight. He's put you in this exact moment and situation for a reason your vision might not be sharp enough to comprehend yet. Humble yourself with *Alif Laam Meem*, and keep going. That's the beauty of Islam: a sincere belief of the Unseen doesn't burden you with worry, it frees you from it.

If you keep trying, and if you keep walking toward Him, remember that He'll run toward you. It just takes that one step, just that one intense desire to kill your pleasure for His own.

We're so blinded by the fear of being seen as a failure in the eyes of society, that the extent of our vision doesn't go past the ideas of what they might see. This confuses us of our intentions and our sole purpose as servants and lovers of God. We lie to ourselves by turning every wrong into a right. Altering Islam to fit our lifestyles instead of developing our lifestyles to fit into the fold of Islam.

Allah (SWT) tells us, "O you who have believed, if you fear Allah, He will grant you a criterion and will remove from you your misdeeds and forgive you. And God is the possessor of great bounty." (The Qur'an, 8:29)

"… He will grant you a criterion."

The word used for 'criterion' in the Arabic language is *furqaan*. It means that He's going to show you how to judge between right and wrong.

God has asked us to fear nothing but Him, and Him alone. These worldly fears that the whisperer tries to divert our attention (toward Him) with — they only distort our intentions, our work, and most definitely our relationship with the Almighty. Our hearts are attached to illusions instead of having a deeper understanding of the required love and fear for our heart's Creator. We keep wanting more and more of what we need less of: attention, numbers, percentages, and comfort, thinking the increase will determine our success and happiness in life. Ah, such is the world of illusions and expectations. Living there only hardens your heart and destroys your soul. It gives you a pain that's been disguised as pleasure, but nothing can be concealed for too long. The Truth always prevails.

Once that pain hits you, channel the negative energy into a love so committed, that it forces your heart to attach to the One who made it. Every other love will be encompassed within your Love for Him, and that's what will determine your success and happiness in this world. That's what will eventually take you to the Next world with an abundance of His blessings showered upon you.

Be fearless when doubts of the future inhibit your mind. Remember that God has everything under control.

YEARNING

Do you ever feel like you're living in a perpetual state of longing, but you can't pinpoint what it is that you're longing for? It's this strange sensation that consumes you with its ambiguity. As the days, months, and years pass, you discover that this longing you feel won't ever really fade away.

You find that no amount of money, fame, or beauty that He gives you can ever diminish your desire for "more." No amount of love from anyone will ever be enough to fill the void within you. That missing piece will always be there.

It's not about all those goals still in the process of being achieved. It's not about how much you want to do, or how overwhelmed you are because of all the knowledge and beauty thrown at you each day. No. This yearning isn't of the material world. The cure to this feeling can't be found here. It's a yearning to meet your Lord, once and for all. The One who made you. The only One who never fails you. This world will never satisfy the ocean within you, so you tire yourself with work, to reach your final destination in peace.

You tire yourself to feel alive.

You're living for the One you love most. Of course, it's hard work. Of course, you'll want to perfect your ways for His pleasure. You'll tire, but you'll live even more. Everything you once knew is redefined: life, love, desire. You're living in a world of illusions and deceit to find the Truth. You fight against the whispers, over and over. Sometimes you'll fail, sometimes you won't. Sometimes you'll want to give up, but your longing for Him and your desire to be more won't let you. Good. Don't let it go. Think runner's high: when you don't experience that high, you're pleased and content with where you're at. When you're compla-cent, you're heedless toward striving for more.

No, keep yearning. Keep working. The work doesn't ever stop — not in this world, at least.

FOR HIS SAKE

I am continually making an effort to use my sadness and anxiety as a means to get closer to the One who put it in my heart. Everything He does, He does for a reason, and how could the One Who created your heart, ever wish for anything but the best for it? Nothing in this life is constant, or steady. There are always bumps and holes along the road. There will always be ups and downs, forcing you to make decisions based on how you deal with hardship. Do you see the bumps and holes from a distance and avoid them? Alternatively, do you cross over them so you can feel the pain and then learn from it, knowing that avoiding them will only stop you from reaching your destination?

You can either submit to your desires or submit to your Lord. You can either take the pain or ignore it. You can either drown in your sorrow or drown in His love.

Remember Him always. Remember that whatever situation you're in now, you're in for a reason that might not be visible to you yet. The best, most beautiful things in life are always the ones that take more effort to find. Use your sadness to find Him, over and over again — there's a new feeling and lesson found each time. Drown in His Love and live in His submission. Keep seeking knowledge. Keep your eyes open. Keep learning from every single situation.

Inevitably, with every hardship comes ease. Be patient, but open your eyes. The beauty of the struggle lies in the battle itself.

STRESS

It's easy to let small issues or discomforts get out of control. You think about everything you need to get done all day long, and then spend little to none of your day doing it, ultimately wearing yourself out. You're subconsciously creating internal chaos when all you're trying to do is find structure and order.

You think about what you need to get done more than you work because you fear you won't get through the initial pain and struggle. But the truth is, you will always get through it. As long as you maintain a steady pace while running and take frequent sips of water, you do not need to fear being out of breath.

You know you've lost your pace when you're constantly being distracted by the flowers lining the sidewalk. You start losing your focus and begin to slow down both mentally and physically. You then start indulging in your desires, whether it's consciously or subconsciously. That's when you know you've lost the battle within. That's when you know your stress has reached a whole new level.

We all have our falls in life — they are the only way we can stand back up. What's important is learning how to deal with those falls every time you do come back up. How do you handle your stress when it gets out of control? Why are thoughts of what you can't do inhibiting your soul?

Have faith in Him so you can have confidence in yourself. Pray. Ask Him to help you get through whatever difficulties you're facing. You must remember that these moments of hardship are just blessings disguised as tests from the Almighty. He's giving you an opportunity to turn to Him. He wants to listen to you, and you need to make it a habit to be speaking to Him.

He's always there for you. Trusting in your Lord is your source of all and any hope.

You can't get rid of stress completely, but you can learn to deal with it. Stop underestimating the limits of your potential, because your potential is truly unlimited. That kind of self-deprecation is just another way of seeing how you fear the uncertainty of your success. Stop doubting yourself and start. Organize your time wisely by making schedules for yourself. If you surrender to God and trust in Him completely, you'll have faith that He's given you more strength than you're aware of. So if you instill this within your heart, the distractions will become more accessible to control. You'll know that God is helping you by giving you the power of inner strength, and now it just depends on how you use it.

Turn to Him to find your peace. Your rest is in His remembrance; don't overexert yourself by failing to be in that remembrance while working. Don't get distracted by the colorful flowers surrounding you while you pace yourself towards your goal, both initial and ultimate. You need to be with Him at all times. Do your part, and He'll do His. Live in the essence of His love and mercy, and patiently persevere.

THE SWEETNESS OF HARDSHIP

Of the many benefits in pondering verses of the Qur'an, gaining the ability to redefine words and ideas has to be the most fulfilling.

The circumstances we deem as hardships are generally based on some form of worldly restriction (i.e. the inability to experience a pleasurable emotion that fulfills any of our humanistic desires). Other times, they're spiritual struggles that tend to endanger our *imaan* (faith), if we give up on our battle against the *Shaytan* and our ego.

Whether the hardship you're experiencing lies in the sacred world or the mundane, it's something that has to be seen in a positive light. While most of the world today strives for instant ease and gratification, ruminators of Qur'anic verses know that with every hardship comes comfort, as Allah (SWT) tells our Prophet (SAW) in the 94th chapter of the Qur'an. Note that He doesn't use the words "before" or "after." No, there will be ease in the depths of our hardship. Perhaps it can be found in the sincerity and love we turn to Him with, or in applying the knowledge our lessons of difficulty teach us. Regardless, the ease does come.

Patience is vital when it comes to embodying a peaceful mindset in the midst of difficulty. That peace can't be achieved solely by enduring the pain, but by putting your complete trust in God with the conviction that He will undoubtedly grant you ease. How? Take a look at Surah al-Furqan, the 25th chapter of the Qur'an. In verses 70-73, Allah (SWT) mentions the one who repents doesn't testify to falsehood, passes by ill speech with dignity, listens when reminded of verses of his Lord, and lastly, asks God to be an example of the righteous and be granted a spouse and children who are the coolness of his eyes.

"Those will be awarded the Chamber for what they patiently endured, and they will be received therein with greetings and [words of] peace."

Some of us see hardship as the result of sins we've committed. We feel like God punishes us in this world in the form of hardship. Maybe He is, but be mindful of the nature of hardship and difficulty in this world. Our Prophet (SAW) said: "O people, repent to your Lord, for verily I seek forgiveness from God and repent to him more than seventy times in a day."

God had already forgiven all his sins, yet he still asked for His forgiveness, and also went through tremendous hardship throughout the course of his life. Interpreting our struggles as punishments subliminally alters our intention(s) when we ask God for forgiveness. Repent, but not with the hopes of being relieved from all hardship. That's what your *du'a* is for, but even then, remember that hardship is inevitable. Ask Him for a stronger back to carry the heavy load. Repent to attain His pleasure and to find *sukoon* (peace) in your heart.

Know that the greatest calamity to befall a human being is his inability to serve God inwardly [i.e. laziness, arrogance, heedlessness] when he is physically capable of doing so. Whether you feel your hardships are sent to you as a blessing or a punishment, make sure you use them as a means to strengthen your faith and build your relationship with Allah. Try to see those hardships through an optimistic and opportunistic lens. This is your chance to turn back to your Lord more firmly than ever before. Go hard at it.

Ibn Qayyim once said, "From the perfection of Allah's *ihsan* (excellence) is that He allows His slave to taste the bitterness of the break before the sweetness of the mend. So He does not break his believing slave, except to mend him. He does not withhold from him, except to give him. So He does not test him (with hardship), except to cure him."

TESTS OF FEAR

Every difficulty we undergo, we associate with some form of loss, whether it is of the material world (money, food, assets) or the spiritual (peace). Every difficulty also incites a feeling of pain or distress — but once you ponder that pain — it subdues, and loss itself becomes the most excellent teacher.

It's important to remember that if those temporary feelings aren't dealt with correctly, your losses will give birth to the most significant loss of all: [the loss of] patience. Allah (SWT) re-affirms this juncture of cause and effect in the second chapter of the Qur'an.

"And We will surely test you with something of fear and hunger and a loss of wealth and lives and fruits, but give good tidings to the patient…" - (The Qur'an, 2:155)

When He (SWT) tests you with political and economic difficulty (fear and hunger), it only gives you an opportunity to channel that fear into a greater fear for Him. Fortunately, He tells you exactly how to do it. In this verse, God first points out the ownership He has over us and all that we deem ours. He then tells us that "the patient will receive good tidings". These few words shed light upon an angle of difficulty and patience we tend to overlook. Instead of dwelling over that difficulty, mapping out a game plan for how to escape from it, or even waiting for it to pass, we are advised to be patient. Also, yes, that means more than just waiting for the storm to pass. Patience comprises of instilling a genuine fear for God in your heart — believing in the Unseen. It means to have sincerity as the sole foundation of your *du'a*, knowing that God surely knows what is best for you. It says to remember that He is the All-Seer, All-Knower, All-Hearer.

It doesn't end there though. God then tells us that when disaster or calamity strikes these patient souls, they say,

"Inna lillahi wa inna ilahi raji'oun." - (The Qur'an, 2:156)

Indeed we belong to Allah, and indeed to Him, we will return.

In these few verses, our entire perception of where we're headed and Who we belong to is put into perspective. God reminds us that our time here is limited by taking away what He's given us, while telling us exactly how to deal with that loss. We learn how to conceptually redefine ownership and what it means to be patient during times of hardship.

Ultimately, the fear God tests us with has only one purpose: [to make us] strengthen and increase our fear for Him. That's how you learn to be patient, and this, in particular, will help you apply your knowledge of Him as your Master and you as His slave, through your inward and outward actions. You'll see it and feel it. You own nothing because He possesses all of you. To Him, you belong, and to Him, you will return. This life is just a passing moment of time. Think about it: how much water does your finger return with after bringing it out of seawater?

Allah (SWT) concludes with the 157th verse. He tells us that those who are patient "will have blessings and mercy sent to them from their Lord, it is those who are the [rightly] guided."

Our scholars of the Qur'an interpret this verse as God commanding angels to make *du'a* for those people.

SubhanAllah. Just imagine that for a moment.

PURSUIT OF IMPACT

When I was younger, I would go to bed every night with a ceiling filled with glow-in-the-dark stars and a pounding heart that couldn't contain its excitement for all the dreams it was dreaming while looking up. I also had an optimistic, naive mind that thought nothing could ever impede my efforts to create an impact in the world and inspire people. Whether it was through using my hands, words, or vision, I knew I would do it somehow.

However, as I grew older, I realized how easy it is to feel discouraged by failure and then unknowingly have your intentions altered. While we should be pursuing impact, we subconsciously begin vying for happiness, money, popularity, and so forth — hedonistic pursuits. The search of impact is all about the people and places around you. It's the most selfless place you can be.

If you study the life of Prophet Nuh (A.S), you'll find that he was on a long-term journey to spread a message, but what resulted was a paucity of progress; only a handful listened to his call. When he encouraged them to ask for His pardon, they thrust their fingers in their ears and drew their cloaks over their heads. What did he do? He continued to preach the Oneness of God without letting failure discourage him. He focused his dedication on his ultimate goal to please Allah, knowing that accurate guidance would only come forth into the hearts of his followers through His will. The distressed and discouraged Nuh (A.S) prayed for Light to overpower the darkness he was experiencing. Despite his profusion of effort coupled with a lack of result, he became one of the most well-respected individuals in the history of Islam. Later prophets ensouled his story and aligned themselves to his legacy.

When our Prophet traveled to Ta'if and invited people to Islam, not a single soul took the *shahadah* (testimony). He was almost stoned; as he fled for safety, Ta'if's sands soaked up the blood from his sandals, from the stones that struck him. The entire journey was seemingly futile. He saw no impact, but in Surah Jinn, the 72nd chapter of the Qur'an, Allah told *Rasullulah* (SAW) that a group of *jinn* passed by him while he was praying, and each one took the *shahadah*. They became prominent preachers of Islam and converted many other *jinn* to the faith, too.

There is beauty in the world of the Unseen — genuinely believing in it, and understanding that there will be an impact in places we aren't aware of.

Sometimes we have to exhaust our potential while remembering that God will never burden us with more than we can bear. Recollect the inspiring thoughts and unbreakable ambition your younger-self had while staring up at those glow-in-the-dark stars. Push through, break the boundaries, and don't settle for mediocrity.

Allah (SWT) tells us, "... And that there is not for man except that [good] for which he strives and that his effort is going to be seen."- (The Qur'an, 53:39-40)

The result is never as important as the efforts we put into reaching it.

CHAPTER THREE: FALL

One-third of the way through, at almost 2,200 feet, Zohra began to lose her breath. The winds were harsh and were making it more and more difficult for her to climb with ease. She felt dizzy and nauseous — she needed to take a break, and she needed water. The ambitious climber began to hallucinate and couldn't remember that the liter of water was in her backpack.

"Oh my god," she exclaimed, dizzily. "What's going on? Where is my water? Where did Tahira go?"

Zohra took a deep breath to calm herself, sat down and reclined her body on the mountain as much as she could. She closed her eyes and made her du'as.

"Ya Allah, give me sukoon (peace)," she whispered. "Help me get out of the mental state I'm in. Give me strength."

She remained in her reclined position and decided to put her trust entirely into God's hands. She waited patiently and then suddenly realized that her liter of water was right next to her, inside her backpack. She wiped the sweat off her forehead and unzipped the top of her bag. Confused at how and why she had become so distraught and mindless, she pulled out the water and chugged almost half of it within a span of 60 seconds.

Then she pulled out her notebook for the first time throughout her journey.

"Oh my god. I just had an anxiety attack. So during it, I remember wondering where Tahira went. That is so disturbing. Why was I feeling dependent on someone else? I should have stayed calm and focused, with my heart in a state of God's remembrance. Before I started this journey, I told myself that I know the journey won't be easy and there will be difficulties — but I will welcome them with

open arms knowing that they are given by God. How did I forget that in a brief moment of stress?" she wrote, disappointed in herself.

Zohra sighed and placed the notebook and pen back into her backpack, each in their respective spots.

At that moment, she felt a pang of loneliness and pain in her heart. The cold wind felt incredibly bitter, and the sky seemed darker than usual. The clouds were heavy, overcoming her with a thick, gut-wrenching gloom.

"Zohra!"

Zohra looked around and couldn't see anyone.

"Zohra!"

She turned her body around and finally saw Tahira walking towards her.

"I've been looking for you! said Tahira. "Where did you go?"

"Oh wow, I was looking for you too," Zohra exclaimed with surprise. "I went through a mini anxiety attack. A few minutes after you went to use the restroom, I felt extremely dizzy and needed water. I got scared because I was alone, and then needed to calm myself by remembering God and writing. That always does the trick."

"You have a beautiful soul, Zohra," Tahira said to her. "I think I got lost too, now that I think about it. The restroom was a ways away, and I thought I came back to where I left you, but I guess not.

The two were then back up and climbing the mountain, this time side by side.

They talked about everything under the sun: their past, their present, and their plans. They were both writers who challenged themselves constantly. They wanted to be full-time writers but were in school for careers that they knew would make their parents happy.

"How do you do this every single week?" Zohra asked Tahira. "I was training for years just to do this on my own."

"You're too afraid of your potential," Tahira said. "You're just like me. I used to be afraid of everything growing up — actually even up until my late teen years."

"So how did you get out of it?"

"I realized how important failure is, and how it's a good thing. And I learned how to put my trust in God's hands completely."

The two climbed some more, in silence. Zohra was thinking about this whole idea of fear and how to battle it. She knew all it took was a shift of mindset and perspective — seeing fear as something positive versus negative.

"Hey, I'm going to let you maintain your pace," Tahira told Zohra. "I'm about to go a little faster, but I'll meet you up there. Don't worry about anything and make sure to stay hydrated."

Zohra nodded and put up a front that she was excited to continue on her own; she knew what Tahira was trying to do, but also knew that she had good intentions.

A few minutes later, Zohra noticed that she was approaching a more difficult part of the mountain. She had to make sure to keep her muscles firm and not be flimsy in her move upwards. As she grabbed onto the rock with her right hand first, her hand happened to slip even though she was keeping it firm and steady. It slipped and snatched, and then Zohra felt a sharp pain in her wrist, almost as if someone brought a knife inside her and cut the inside of her wrist off.

Zohra shrieked at the top of her lungs. She knew no one was around to help, but she had to release her pain in some form. At *that moment, heavy rain began to pour, and Zohra was in a state of extreme discomfort.*

She didn't know if she could continue her journey, but she decided to push through and keep her thoughts as positive as possible. She used her left hand to climb up a few more steps until she found a place to sit and rest. Soon her vision was suffused with green shrubs, orange and red Indian paintbrush flowers, and a small, steady-flowing waterfall. At this point, Zohra was utterly exhausted, but her heart was full because of all the beauty surrounding her. She sat down and took a deep sigh of relief.

"SubhanAllah," she said. She pulled a small bottle of Arnica oil to massage into her wrist.

FALLING

The hardest part about falling is keeping your eyes open. You're caught in a web of chaos, but all you can do is calm your heart and wait to be released. You watch everything with sharp eyes inside your pounding heart. Pure observation. Pure reflection. Pure submission. You take your fears of what's to come to Him, building a shield of His protection around you. You extract the lessons from your fall and leave the rest behind, separating the calm from the chaos.

If you think you're wasting your time, you aren't reminding yourself to implement the lessons learned for future walks and runs. You're too worried about stopping yourself from the inevitable, too afraid of an inability to get back up.

However, when you're falling, you can't control your fall. You can only manage how you'll deal with it afterward. Will you learn from your mistakes or become arrogant? Will you stand up stronger or weaker?

Use your eyes and relax your heart, and then find what produced your friction with gravity. Just watch and learn. You're subconsciously preparing for the next fall.

The hardest part is observing, reflecting, and humbling yourself. After that, you have to decide how to get back up. Do you absorb the pain or let it seep through to your heart and soul? Do you channel the pain into decisive action or allow it to create a prolonged stagnancy?

Your test is whether or not you stand up with more inner strength and more faith in Him. It's not about your fears; it's about using those fears to submit to Him, asking Him to protect you and guide you.

Ask Him for protection, guidance, strength, willpower — whatever it is you need — and then trust that He'll give it to you. Trust that He'll keep you safe, and then build your strength off that trust. When you sharpen your vision and break through the surface, you'll find the invisible buried underneath what seemed like layers and layers of visible. You'll find a love so pure; a truth so clear.

When you're falling, time becomes abstract. It loses all substance and feeling is the only thing you know. Your observation, reflection, submission, and then ultimately your strength is rooted from sense. Feel His light. His unconditional love. He'll be waiting for you to turn to Him after every fall, yearning to help you back up every single time.

UNDERSTANDING QADAR

When you're distanced from something you hold dear to you, you can either dwell in your sorrow, or you can ponder the workings of distance and removal in itself.

A loss is a beautiful blessing in disguise.

Skim through the pages of Surah al-Baqarah, and you'll find that God touches on the relationship between loss and patience. He says: "And We will surely test you with something of fear and hunger and a loss of wealth and lives and fruits, but give good tidings to the patient, Who, when disaster strikes them, say, "Indeed we belong to Allah, and indeed to Him, we will return." - (The Qur'an, 2:156)

When God tests you with political and economic difficulty (fear and hunger), it only gives you an opportunity to channel that fear into a more significant concern for Him. Fortunately, He tells you exactly how to do it. In this verse, Allah (SWT) first points out the ownership He has over us, and all that we deem ours. He then tells us that "the patient will receive good tidings." Instead of mapping out a game plan for how to escape from your difficulties or stagnantly wait for them to pass, we're advised to be patient.

Yes, that means much more than just waiting for the storm to pass you by. A bigger part of it is believing in the Unseen. It's how you find sincerity and trust in your *du'a*, knowing that God surely knows what's best for you.

He (SWT) then tells us that when disaster strikes these patient souls, they say, "*Inna lillahi wa inna ilahi raji'oun.*" Indeed we belong to Allah, and indeed to Him, we will return.

In these few verses, our entire perception of where we're headed and Whom we belong to is put into perspective. He reminds us that our time here is limited by taking away what He's given, while telling us exactly how to deal with that loss. We learn how to redefine ownership and what it means to be patient during times of hardship.

Another note: the word He uses for "disaster" in this verse is *musibah*. This word, un-coincidentally, shares the same root as the word *asabah*, meaning to shoot someone with an arrow. So, this *musibah* that God mentions to us is one that comes from Him and hits exactly on point. Think *tawakkul* (trust in God). Think reliance on Allah, and belief in *qadar* (fate). In Surah at-Talaq, He reminds us of these three elements of belief. He gives us solace through His ultimate promise: "Whoever fears God — He will make for him a way out. And will provide for him from where he does not expect. And whoever relies upon God — then He is sufficient for him. Indeed, God will accomplish His purpose. God has already set for everything to an [decreed] extent." - (The Qur'an, 65:2-3)

Often, His decree enters our path uninvited and appears in many guises but, only the *mu'min* (believer) embraces it with a smile and open arms. One of the Prophet Muhammad (SAW)'s companions, 'Urwa ibn az-Zubair, perfectly demonstrated this concept of embracing Allah's decree. While having his leg amputated, he was given the news that one of his four sons died. In light of losing a loved one and a limb, 'Urwa said: "O Allah! You took one child and left me many. You took one organ from my body and left me many organs. O, Allah! You tested me with my body, and you were kind to leave me with good health. You tested me with the loss of my son, but you were kind in leaving me the rest of my children."

Ultimately, the fear our Lord tests us with only encourages us to increase our *tawakkul* and strengthen our *taqwa* (fear of God) and *imaan* (faith). You learn how to live in a constant state of *Alhamdulilah*. No matter what the circumstance may be, you give all your praises to the Most High.

DISTRACTING WHISPERS

Mental clarity is essential as you venture to tackle any task. When you have trouble grasping that clarity, it's because you think you're losing in your fight against desire. The whispers encroach the door of your heart. You're exhausted and distraught. Distracted to the height of extreme frustration.

In this moment you have to be strong. Don't give up out of mere discouragement. Don't just plunge into your lustful desires thinking that the plunge will be your escape. These desires are insatiable. You'll only gain a temporary satisfaction that later turns into a constant pain.

It's so easy to change into that hot dress you've saved for your 'ladies-only' events and hit the nearest club. It's easy to message or call up a cute guy or girl and "wind down" as you two chat. You can even satisfy [one realm] of lustful desires by browsing through provocative images for some eye-candy. The *Shaytan* whispers these exciting thoughts to us in our most vulnerable states. When it comes down to temptation, he doesn't tire in his efforts to lead us astray.

So, what do you do? Make *wudhu* (ablution), pray, and pick up the Qur'an to read and ponder over. There's a verse in the Qur'an that caters to every possible source of distress that visits man. There's a pearl of hidden wisdom behind every word and its placement, so to repel the evil thought, you have to first learn about the whisperer and his devious ways.

God asks us to seek refuge in Him "from the evil of the retreating whisperer - Who whispers [evil] into the breasts of mankind."- (The Qur'an, 114:4-5)

Zoom in on the fourth verse:

مِن شَرِّ الْوَسواسِ الخَنَّاسِ

Min sharri al waswasal khannas

The word *al-waswas* is mentioned in adjective form rather than verb, indicating the persistence of *Shaytan's* whispering. The word *silsilah* translates to "a series of mountains — one after another," alluding to continuity and repetition. Finally, *al khannas* translates to the one who "retreats or steps back, continuously."

There's a recurring message of continuity being conveyed to us here. *Shaytan* is persistent in his efforts to tempt us. After all, he is the accursed whisperer, so how could he ever tire of whispering? That's why we have to work even harder in turn.

While *Shaytan* has the power to reverberate at our chests with his whispers, the ability to remember God is in our hands, and that remembrance — silent or audible, as long as it's sincere — won't let the whisperer penetrate our hearts. His power falters at the gates of *dhikr* (remembrance of God). Sa'id Ibn Jubayr narrates from Ibn Abbas: "*Shaytan* plants himself right above the heart of the son of Adam (A.S). As soon as the son of Adam (A.S) becomes lackadaisical, or heedless and forgetful, *Shaytan* starts whispering. As soon as he remembers Allah, *Shaytan* takes a step back." (Tafsir Ibn Kathir)

THE SWEETEST PAIN

I think we all grow to love loss. When you lose what you've subconsciously been holding on to to feed your ego, you realize how delusional you were in thinking you acquired humble characteristics. It's the sweetest pain to finally see your vision turn from an illusion to reality; from the love of this world to the Creator of it.

It's like God wants you to learn from your arrogance and pride. You've been put here to be tested on how well you can live in His remembrance, so that you can find a better life There. You're taking what seems to be the test an eternity, forgetful of how it's just a passing moment. You don't even know when your last day may be. That reminder serves as a foundation for the fear that needs to be instilled within, of standing before your Lord, with nothing but your deeds.

God takes things away from you so you can find your way back to Him. Your losses in this world are the most beautiful gifts you will ever receive. Use them to see yourself as He does — in your rawest form — stripped of all the money, fame, beauty, or lineage that you measure your worth with. Humble yourself knowing you are merely a servant of God striving to live in His remembrance.

Use your losses to find Him again.

You're an entity with a soul in need of constant purification. Focus on the beauty of your soul first. Everything else we deem beautiful in this world is just an illusion; it's a passing enjoyment. So with that knowledge, you'll gain the vision to see that what you amount to is measured by nothing but the Love and Light within.

He knows exactly what you need to fall back onto the straight path, miles away from pride, keeping your heart and mind subconsciously absorbed in the Hereafter. Be grateful for your losses, for they are the one of the greatest blessings.

ALIF LAAM MEEM

Alif Laam Meem. Some things are only meant for God to know.

Whether it's your hardship or another's, know that God is the Best of Planners, the All-Hearer, All-Knower, the Most Wise, the Most Merciful. There's a reason you're going through this particular hardship. Perhaps He wants to test the extent of your *taqwa* (fear of God).

How much do you fear and love your Lord? How will you handle this seemingly unfortunate situation? Will you walk toward Him or move further away?

Allah (SWT) tells us in the last verse of the second chapter that He "does not charge a soul except [with that within] its capacity." - (The Qur'an, 2:286)

Find solace in His promise. The pain and obstacles that befall you are only tools to keep your heart close to Allah. If dealt with appropriately, you'll find that they're just lessons made to learn from. Once you extract those lessons and turn to Allah instead of turning away, you'll see exactly what you need to channel pain that harms you, into an illness that heals and helps. You'll feel it. Maybe you'll start repenting much more than you usually would. It's almost like He's calling out to you, asking you to talk to Him and ask for forgiveness for all your sins, from smallest to most prominent, known and unknown. (Note: Do you realize what a precious blessing this is? He's giving you the opportunity to ask for forgiveness. The fact that our hearts are still alive, and our tongues can move to call out to Him is a blessing in itself.)

We were born as and will forever be slaves of Allah, made to worship Him. Use your entire being to follow His law. That includes your heart, your mind, and your tongue. Know that ease comes with hardship, and there are hidden blessings in pain that only reveal themselves later on. All beautiful results initially undergo a set of trials and tribulations.

And remember, it's a two-way street. You can either remain stagnant or keep moving forward, because if you're not moving, you're not going anywhere.

"And when waves come over them like canopies, they supplicate Allah, sincere to Him in religion. However, when He delivers them to the land, there are [some] of them who are moderate [in faith]. And none rejects Our signs except everyone treacherous and ungrateful." - (The Qur'an, 31:32)

So, remember, keep moving forward. Regardless of how "bad" your situation may be, let *Alhamdulilah* resonate in your heart. Open your eyes and find gratefulness for all the gifts He's given you. Use your hardships to go harder on yourself. Improve the quality of your worship. Increase your level of *khushu* (softness of the heart) to perfect your *salah* (prayer). Learn the art of *tadabbur* in all of its entirety. There's a phrase used in the Qur'an, *Haqqa Tilawatih* (Rightful Recitation), that refers to this act of *tadabbur*.

Tadabbur isn't *tajweed* (rules when reciting the Qur'an) or the means of purification one should observe before reciting the Qur'an. It's about contemplating Allah's words and examining their inner meanings. Then, acting on them.

Let's relive the time of those Hasan Al-Baṣri once mentioned: "Certainly, those that came before you saw the Qur'an as personal letters from their Lord; hence, they contemplated it during the night, and acted upon it during the day."

Strengthen your family ties through love and *du'a*. Make sacrifices for them without expecting anything in return, because that's what love is all about — paying no heed to how much you're being loved or cared for, if at all, because you know your love isn't ultimately for his/her sake alone.

The goal is to never lose sight of your ultimate test. Everything God blesses you with in this world (good or bad) is a test of how you deal with it. And the only way to find your way out of any difficulty isn't through it, but always through Him.

HIDDEN REWARDS

You know those moments when you work so hard for something but ultimately feel like giving up, because you don't think your work is worthy? You abandon your motivation, and a wave of exhaustion takes its place.

Those are the saddest moments — draining you of your energy and leaving you with indescribable pain. When you reflect upon these moments retrospectively, you note that the pain was utterly self-inflicted: it was a result of your forgetfulness.

You forgot to remember that this hard work isn't for your grade. The hours you're spending studying for this test are just a part of a more significant test: this life itself. All your tests, big or small, are encompassed by His own.

So the aim isn't to do good but to do right here, to find a better place There. The objective isn't about enduring the struggle while you climb the mountain, but rather the closeness you develop with your Lord in the midst of that struggle.

The pain you feel now will be the peace you feel tomorrow. Blood, sweat, and tears are critical elements of any masterpiece, visible or invisible. Patience, perseverance, and prayer are vital elements to all success, visible or invisible.

"And be patient, for indeed, God does not allow to be lost the reward of those who do good." - (The Qur'an, 11:115)

Even if you think your hard work won't reveal the way you want it to, know that God is the Seer of all that you do. As long as you're attempting to utilize your full potential and work with His remembrance, you have to trust that He's pleased. Trust that He wants to help you succeed.

Seek refuge in patience and prayer, and then reflect on your perspective towards work. Maybe you need a break to reset and refresh, gaining a new perspective which forces you to see things differently.

Have optimism and find solace in God's words. In Surah al-Kahf, we read the words *"Aasa an yahdiyani rabbee li `aqraba min hatha"* — "Perhaps, my Lord will guide me to what is nearer than this." - (The Qur'an, 18:24)

What is meant by "this" — the word *hatha*? It's the next step in your journey — not the external one, but the one which grants you strength, understanding, closeness to Him, and hidden rewards.

While in the midst of your journey — you can either look up at all that's left and subsequently feel overwhelmed, clouded, and doubtful — or you can make a conscious effort to take it step by step, trusting that there is a Divine reason you're on this path, pacing yourself toward your destination. Try to appreciate and understand God's wisdom behind each moment, even the most difficult ones: when you're parched of thirst and are unable to quench it immediately; when your knees feel weak, but you have to keep climbing to stay on track; when you feel desolate, within and without, desperate for company as you tread alone. The struggle teaches you patience and grants you an immense reward. So be patient, and watch as He blesses you with wholesome abundance.

AN ENDLESS BATTLE

The sadness that resides within sinning is only found after you sin. You realize that your worst enemy has defeated you. The pain you feel is inevitable, so instead of ignoring it, you learn from it. You go back and try to figure out where your limbs started feeling weak. You see where you began to fall, and you always find that it was a sadness that led to an even greater sorrow. It's like you tried filling your holes with water, forgetting that the dirt will only absorb the liquid.

There's an emptiness inside all of us that we try to fill by either submitting to our desires or submitting to His word. We have hopes and a purpose. Unlike angels who have no desire, we're always fighting against our *nafs* (ego). We're continually trying to deem anything that disturbs the peace of our heart, an enemy.

It seems like life in this world is an endless battle between man and *Shaytan*. To defeat him, you have to learn his tricks and study his ways. Know him well. The thoughts he's always trying to feed you with are the biggest curse you'll ever face. He wants you to lose hope in the sins you commit, and forget that you were born a sinner, made to repent. His goal is to ultimately have you drown in the same arrogance he immersed himself in. At some point, your heart will surely darken, and faith will start to dissipate, but that's when you tire yourself with repentance, and with the *du'a* of having your faith renewed. The key is not to lose hope, and not to fall under his curse. That's the only way we can begin each journey of purifying our souls of filth.

Sins give birth to the greatest sadness, and then the saddest joy. They have a way of taking us back to God, which equates to them being the greatest blessing in disguise. This battle we're fighting is what we were made human for. The pain will strengthen you and the lessons learned will sharpen your vision. When the two combine — experiences and pain — you will be able to implement the knowledge you gained the next time you feel weak.

The most beautiful and substantive things in life are always the ones that cannot be seen. Knowledge is one of them. It's a Light that God places inside our souls so we can connect everything we see, feel, and know — to keep finding Him. His guidance is our greatest gift.

An endless battle that consists of falls, cuts, and bruises, only results in an infinite journey of standing stronger, cleansing the wounds, and letting the injuries heal.

Allahumma innaka 'afuwwun tuhibul 'afwa fa'fu 'anni.

"Oh Allah, certainly You are Most Forgiving, You love to forgive, so forgive me."

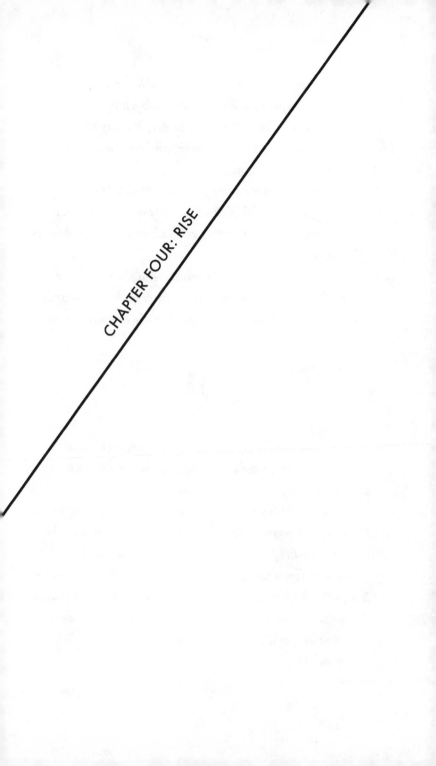

CHAPTER FOUR: RISE

It had been an hour since she last massaged her wrist — it was still in pain of course, but she knew it was slowly getting better.

Zohra was now more than two-thirds of the way up the mountain. Physically — she was exhausted, and her muscles felt sore — but mentally — she felt grateful.

As she reflected on her journey, she was reminded that she made it this far only because of God. She was put in such difficult situations, but in retrospect, the difficulties were made easy for her without any effort on her part.

She was on an uncomfortable journey — a place that was outside her comfort zone. She was forced to understand the true meaning of patience. She was forced to learn how to make difficult decisions on her own.

Zohra took another break to massage her wrist with some Arnica oil. She sat down, pulled out the bottle from her backpack, and in an instant, a bright blue bird flew onto her hand.

She was about to panic, but in a millisecond of time, she remembered from her previous experience on the mountain to stay calm. So she did and softly exhaled the breath she was holding.

The bird began licking Zohra's wrist with its 2cm long tongue. It would lick, then look up at Zohra, and then start licking again. She had never seen a bird like this before — it looked like something from another world. She had also never seen a wild bird lick a human hand.

Confused but somehow at ease, Zohra let the bird do what it was doing for the few moments before it flew away.

"Woah, what the heck was that!" she said, in awe and dismay.

Some things weren't for her to answer.

She moved her wrist around in a circular motion, and it felt the same as it did before the bird licked it. She pulled out the Arnica oil again and massaged it into the area in pain. Then, she pulled out her notebook and tried writing a bit with her left hand.

"A bright blue bird just flew onto my hand and started licking my wrist. It was crazy, but even more so is the fact that I didn't freak out. I stayed calm and allowed it to finish whatever it was doing. When it flew away, I thought that maybe my wrist would feel somewhat different, but no. It felt the same. But maybe it will heal sooner than it would have if the bird didn't lick it like that. I'm not sure. Also not sure what kind of bird that was but it seemed like some Godsend."

Zohra paused and looked up. She realized the sun was going to set in less than two hours, and she wanted to make it to the top to witness it. She put away her notebook and got back on her feet again.

Throughout her climb, Zohra took good care of her wrist. She made sure not to put too much strain on it and instead, put more weight onto her left hand.

And then she kept climbing and didn't stop for a while.

She was focused, but reflecting throughout.

As she was about to reach another rest area, she saw a tall figure moving in the distance.

"Wait, is that Tahira?" she asked herself.

"TAHIRA!" she yelled.

Tahira turned, and her face was beaming with the brightest smile.

"Hey! I knew I'd see you up here!" she replied. "How has the climb been so far?"

Zohra filled her in on everything, from her wrist getting sprained to the bright blue bird licking it.

"Woah, definitely sounds like a crazy adventure," said Tahira. "I'm proud of you for handling all that on your own."

Tahira then began to share what her journey was like for the past few hours that the two were solo. She had a way of telling stories that Zohra admired. From the way she described imagery to the way she would incorporate subtle metaphors into her verbally shared stories — it was inspiring for Zohra.

As they wrapped up their exchange of experiences, Tahira told Zohra that she was going to take a nap at the rest stop, wake up to pray Maghrib and Isha, and then sleep there for the night.

"Do you do that often?" Zohra asked her.

"I do this maybe once a month when I'm just having more trouble than usual while climbing. Don't worry, I'm fine," she said.

Zohra wasn't sure if Tahira was acting this way to make her feel like she's capable of doing more than she thought, or if Tahira was just exhausted.

It was another one of those things that weren't meant for her to answer.

"Ah, okay," Zohra sighed under her breath. "Well, I had some incredible conversations with you. I don't know if I'll see you again, but I want to thank you for everything. You might not realize it, but you were a huge part of my journey here. I learned a lot from you."

"I learned a lot from you too, believe it or not." Tahira smiled and then turned to rest.

DEEP CLEANING

Have you ever looked at your life in retrospect, thinking about the many situations God put you into — situations you didn't understand at the time — only to bring you to a much better place?

You think about the phases you've gone through and the stages you've reached in the hierarchy of spiritual growth. You think about the way you approached certain situations and how you interacted with certain people. You think about all the ways you helped yourself get closer to Him, and all the ways you pushed yourself away.

All this thinking and analyzing, sometimes, it drives you crazy. There's one thing though, that brings you pain so immense, no other memory of your past comes even close. It's the memory of your sins. But you only accept those sins (and the pain) because you've learned to embrace the decree of Allah.

In Ibn al-Qayyim's book, *Tareeq-al-Hijratayn*, he mentions this divine decree and wisdom of Allah. He indicates how God allows a person to sin while He can protect that person from it, for reasons only He knows. Qayyim mentions one of these reasons in his book.

"One of the *salafs* (early generation) said: A person may commit a sin and enter Paradise because of it, or he may do a righteous deed and enter Hell because of it. They said: How is that? He said: He commits a sin, then keeps thinking of it, and when he remembers it, he regrets it, feels sorry, beseeches Allah, hastens to erase it and feels broken-hearted and humble before his Lord. That removes self-admiration and pride from him. Alternatively, he may do a good deed, then keep thinking of it, talking about it, feeling proud of it and feeling arrogant because of it, until he enters Hell." (p. 169-172)

Whenever you feel confused as to why you were put into a particular situation or why you weren't strong enough to find a way out of that sin, first think of your shortcomings, and then remember His mercy. God doesn't grant a *mu'min* (believer) Heaven just because of the sin he repented for, but also because of the fear of Allah's wrath that was placed in the heart of that *mu'min*, through that sin.

If the fear and worry aren't there, the repentance isn't sincere. You always have to go back to the Source.

When you look at your life in retrospect, you'll inevitably be reminded of the good, the bad, and the ugly. Those memories serve as reminders of how you'll keep growing. They show you how your life is a never-ending journey of rectifying your wrongs and finding Him over and over again, here, to finally be with Him There.

When you think of all the people who came into your life to either teach you something that would help you on your journey, or to tread on it with you, be grateful for them. Wish them the best in this world and the Next. Free your heart of all anger, animosity, and doubt.

The biggest lesson to take away when memories of past sins begin to surface is never to get too comfortable with where you are. Never feel like you're set. You will always be a sinner, so instead of working on sinning less, first work on repenting more. Instead of thinking you have a pure heart, know that the filth will always be there. You'll still have a heavy load to carry, but your shoulders will get stronger.

Be regular with your moments of solitude. The moments where you remove all thoughts from your mind and look into your heart, letting the *noor* (light) of Allah descend into it, cleansing it of all impurities. Let it call out to Him. Surely, you'll remember displeasing situations from your past, but this is how the process begins. It's the process of deep cleaning. You can't just wipe; you have to scrub vigorously. All the superficial layers will come out with ease, but it takes time for the dirt that's hardened underneath to be removed.

The same goes for the heart, so you have to clean regularly. The intensity of your pain won't lessen — instead, your heart will get stronger.

STROKES OF FAITH

God and His Supreme Wisdom never fail to amaze me.

Ya *Rabb*, how do You mend this broken heart of mine, over and over again? How do You stop the twisting and turning? How do You give me so much ease alongside my difficulties? How do You grab my heart and turn it towards You?

These are the questions I ask my Lord while I ingest my daily dose of *Alhamdulilahs*.

You know you'll go through hardship upon hardship in life. And sometimes you'll envision a particular one as a punishment from your Lord, for all your past or presently accumulating sins. No, these hardships are the most precious blessings you'll be given in this world, and you'll only understand them when examined in hindsight.

They remind you of what you forget to remember: Him. You're not working hard enough to shine His light at the right spots and rectify your wrongs.

Have you ever looked at a freshly painted wall in a dim-lit room? You'll think it looks perfect at first glance. You won't see many imperfections until a high-beam light shines on it. Then, to your surprise, the bumps and dents become visible. Even the color of the paint changes, right?

The painted wall is your heart, and that light is like your eyes. You'll find that light through following the *Sunnah* of our Prophet (SAW), being in the company of those who follow his Sunnah, and through *dhikr* (remembrance) of Allah. Your vision isn't hazy anymore. You've painted your heart with *imaan*, and now, with your sharp vision, you see the defects.

MENDER OF HEARTS

Surely, God is *Al-Jabbar*, the mender of all hearts. Surely, He is the best to create. Your heart can be completely shattered, and He will blend its pieces so swiftly, so gently — that you will forget it was ever broken.

You'll forget the pain because of the ease He granted you through it. You'll learn that anything broken can be fixed. You'll see how that temporary pain created the foundation for internal peace, your sanctuary, in Him and His beautiful attributes.

His mercy is infinite, and we should humble ourselves in gratitude by living within the susurrus of *Alhamdulilah*, in our hearts and our minds, no matter what the situation. We're undeserving of these bounties of love God showers upon us.

He (SWT) is the mender of all hearts, and admittedly, what's lost is always replaced with what is greater.

SIMPLE LOVE

Why do we make love complicated when it's so simple?

It is *so* simple.

But we can't define it in words or actions — its existence is rooted from the language of feeling.

Sometimes it's hidden, sometimes it's disguised, but it's always there. It's everywhere and in everything.

Love is in the perfect moment you lower your head and heart, and place your forehead on the ground in humility. Your entire body declares, "O Allah, glory be to You, the Most High." Love is the enlightenment that feels almost tangible when you rely on nothing but Him and His word. It's in the awareness of all love being encompassed by His greater love and mercy.

It's in the dreams you dream, and the work you do to turn those dreams into reality. It's in silent reflection and loud observation. Love is the sparkle in his eyes, the light in her heart, the affection in touch.

Love is even in pain and struggle. It's in the climb, the failure, and the lesson. Love is primarily in that lump-in-the-throat sadness that sometimes turns into millions of tears.

However, love is simple. You just have to channel its bad into good, like any other feeling. You have to use it in ways it can benefit you and those around you, spreading even greater love. You'll feel internally revived by how simple, yet powerful love is. You'll crave the feeling when it's not there. You'll want to keep strengthening your passion.

You don't strengthen the feeling through words or actions though. You enhance it by holding on to your ties with the One who created that love and placed it in your heart. The depth of your love for Him dictates your passion for any of His creation. When your love for Him increases, the pure love your heart knows becomes a more purified, simple love.

You'll know your love is pure when you feel your heart opening. Your heart opens so it can be purified. And it gets clarified so you can see clearly, with an unwavering focus to grow in this world, while growing closer to Him. All the unnecessary background noise becomes peripheral. All the invisible becomes visible. You'll find love everywhere and in everything.

INSPIRATION

I love being able to feel another person's passion. The most passionate people usually have the strongest, most far-reaching rays of light that pierce you all the way to your heart. They squeeze through every dark crack and fissure, slowly liberating you from your own darkness. They free you from the chaos outside, and pave a path to escape into the peace and tranquility deep within you — a feeling discernible only when you go to Him.

This person's light takes you to Him.

It's like getting a taste of His goodness. He's blessed you with the honor of crossing paths with this person whose light lifts you, takes you away from the filth of this world and ultimately takes you back to its Source: the Creator of all creation. The Creator of all feelings, all beings, and all connection between feeling and being.

SOURCES

You ever wonder if it's possible to love something or someone without getting attached?

You've always been told not to get attached, but how do you practice detachment?

Start with analyzing your thoughts and reflexes. Look at your life in retrospect; think about what made you feel the desire to attach to that person or thing. What made you feel like there was space inside your heart? You'll almost always find the same answer — a lack of contentment within yourself. The discontentment only led you to feel incomplete, worthless, and lonely later on. Within you, there were fictitious emotions enshrouding the Truth, making you believe that another person or thing can fill up the empty spaces. But how could your equal, another human being, fill the emptiness when you can't yourself? You think feeling discontent is the source of your faults and failures, making you vulnerable to anyone or anything that tells you you're not faulty. That feeling is just the cause of distance between you and the Almighty. He's the Mender of Broken Hearts — the only One who can complete you and ease your loneliness. His word is the only thing that has the power to govern your worth.

All praise is due to the Almighty for granting us the gift of such a beautiful Book. We're taught how to live our lives while being constantly reminded of the Exalted, the Absolute Ruler.

"To Him belongs what is in the heavens and what is on the earth, and what is between them, and what is under the soil." - (The Qur'an, 20:6)

How ironic is it that we're ready to love the rain before the clouds? We're ready to attach to the tranquility and sweetness, before connecting to the source of those sensations. Close your eyes and see Him with the eyes of your heart, everywhere.

You think this person or thing, whatever you attach yourself to, is giving you happiness. You think they're completing you because they are your "other half," but these feelings are provided to you by Him; look at them as blessings. Don't fall into those ditches of plausible lies, because once you're in too deep, you'll forget how the Truth feels. True contentment can only be found in the depths of pleasing Him. You'll find peace in His pleasure. You have to learn to love Him so you can love His creation with a pure heart; that's when a detachment from everything but Him will come to you naturally. So no, this doesn't mean you'll never know how to love another person; you'll learn how to love on an entirely different level. You'll see how your love is rooted in the utmost respect for that person. When the object of your love is pure, you'll always find His love in its depths. Attach to nothing but Him and trust that He'll take care of you. Always look for the Source. You'll find yourself at the same place every time.

SPIRITUAL REJUVENATION

Faith, or *imaan*, like all things in life, can never remain stagnant. It's always moving— sometimes at a high, sometimes at a low. Realizing that is the first step to increasing your *imaan* as a whole, and then ultimately keeping it at a somewhat steady level.

The journey never ends though, and it takes a lot of hard work, patience, and persistence.

Imagine your body for a minute. If you don't nourish it with vitamin and mineral-rich foods that it demands for excellence, or if you deprive (or over-exert) your muscles of physical activity, your body and its functions will reflect those poor decisions. You'll fall sick much easier than one who has a nutritious diet and exercises to boost immunity further.

In the same way, when we don't nourish our hearts with that undying, incomparable-to-any-of-creation type of love for Allah, our level of *imaan* tends to reflect a lack of nourishment. Our hearts become sick.

Illness of the body and disease of the heart have the same mental side effects: feelings of suffocation, frustration, and pain. When the illness is a result of poor decision-making skills or a lack of discipline, those negative feelings only escalate. We develop a sense of disappointment that's rooted in putting ourselves into a situation that God has explicitly told us how to avoid.

Allah (SWT) tells us, "Then let man consider [the nature] of his food." - (The Qur'an, 80:24)

Be mindful of how you're treating your body; don't be heedless. Not only does this please your Lord, but the act itself gives you an opportunity to practice self-discipline as well as control your *nafs* (ego). It helps you to enhance and refine your self-respect because you're mindful of what you're putting into your body.

When you're at a spiritual low, one of the best things to do is free yourself from the invisible chains of desire you've wrapped yourself up in. We're slaves to our wishes as human beings. Adopt a more mindful attitude — not only toward what your meals consist of, but toward every thought that crosses your mind to eventually become an action. Imam al-Ghazali always referred to the stomach and reproductive organs as the dominators of desires. When the two are under control, it's less of a hassle to gauge where exactly you and your limbs rest in harmony with His word.

When you're taking care of your body for His sake, you're taking care of your soul. When you feel like you're at a spiritual low and in need of cleansing your heart, start with your body first. Learn how to control your *nafs*. Learn how to detach yourself from the illusion of pleasures in this world, so you can submit to Him instead of your desires.

HIJAB

I often see some of the most beautiful fundamentals of Islam portrayed in such an unpleasant demeanor.

Parents ask their daughters to don the *hijab* (headscarf) without thinking twice about presenting it as an opportunity rather than a responsibility. The same thing goes for husbands, siblings, and friends. Rather than glorifying the *hijab* in all of its entirety, they tend to state 'reasons' (as a means to convince) that typically revolve around not flaunting one's beauty, so that men outside can control themselves. Interesting, because before the *hijab* was mentioned in the Qur'an, God had already told the believing men to lower their gazes, regardless of what kind of clothing a woman chooses to adorn herself with.

The *hijab* is not just a piece of cloth that covers your hair and conceals your beauty. It has a strange way of making you appear even more beautiful. There's no benefit in putting all our energy into trivial matters that revolve around making sure not a single strand of our hair can be seen. If we encourage that kind of mindset, I'm not sure if women, *hijabi* or not, will ever be able to truly appreciate the beauty of *hijab*.

I remember going through a phase of extreme confusion and uncertainty when deciding whether I should start wearing the *hijab* or not. I wasn't quite sure if the *hijab* is obligatory, because of my ignorance toward His words. I hated how a *hijabi* woman is considered more religious than a non-*hijabi* woman (in the eyes of many), and because of that, I felt this dire need to show people that you can be a good, practicing Muslim without necessarily wearing the *hijab*. I found the stereotypes that both Muslims and non-Muslims would associate with the *hijab* extremely frustrating. I ultimately started questioning whether the *hijab* would even have any positive impact on my life and my relationship with God. My friends would try persuading me, being *hijabi* themselves, but their reasons were never convincing enough.

In Surah an-Nur, God commands women "to wrap [a portion of] their head-covers over their chests..." - (The Qur'an, 24:31)

The theme of this *surah* is Light, and the passage of Light mentioned in the *surah* is a spiritual one. Its words illustrate what exactly preserves that Light, which is interesting since Surah an-Nur is known for its rulings. This only implies that if we don't abide by the injunctions mentioned, we'll undergo spiritual problems.

What kind of injunctions are mentioned? The ones that relate to controlling our *nafs*, or ego. I think that's incredible. How we control our desires is directly correlated with our spiritual well-being. This is what drew me in toward the idea of (once and for all) putting on the *hijab*. I think the sole purpose of our existence revolves around how much effort we put into purifying our hearts. In Surah Ash-Shu'ara, Allah reminds us of, "The Day when there will not benefit [anyone] wealth or children, but only one who comes to God with a sound heart." - (The Qur'an, 26:88-89)

The Light is in our hearts, and the beauty of *hijab* has more to do with cultivating that Light, and less with covering our hair. So, what is our sole intention when taking the *hijab*? Increasing our level of faith and working on spiritual well-being. God explores the various facets of modesty and their relationship with our *imaan* (faith) in this surah, as well as morality and how it can interfere with our spirituality. Don't worry about proving to others that you can be a practicing Muslim woman with or without wearing the *hijab*, social stigma, stereotypes, labels, your appearance (seriously, stop worrying about whether you look better with or without *hijab*), and whether or not it will be of any benefit to you.

Know what you're doing and why you're doing it. Strive to attain a sound heart by fulfilling your obligatory duties (seen as opportunities rather than responsibilities; find the beauty first), and disregard all trivial matters that revolve around the opinion of others.

Always question your intentions and keep them in check. And know that when you do something for God with a sincere intention to come nearer to Him, He will surely guide you and ease your difficulties.

CHAPTER FIVE: SUMMIT

From a distance, Zohra could see orange-yellow rays of light creeping through the clouds above. Something was telling her she was close to the top, but she didn't know for sure yet. She didn't want to believe it.

She began struggling to climb. She was thirsty and slightly dizzy — but still felt content. She paused for a minute and sat down, quenching her thirst using the last bit of water in her backpack — but at this point, she wasn't worried. She knew God had her back, for He had brought her to this point through His Greatness.

When she got up, Zohra was nervous. She didn't even want to make it to the top because of how much she began enjoying the process of getting there, instead. But she could see the top of the mountain now. Tears started streaming down her face.

"Am I dreaming?" she said. "This is so surreal."

Zohra took three more steps and found herself overlooking the city of Bozeman. Everything looked so miniscule, reminding her of all the struggles she faced. What was greater was all that she learned because of those struggles.

She stood there, in awe, and then pulled out her notebook. She dated the page "January 2, 2012" and began to write. This time, she used her right hand. Perhaps, the bright blue bird was a Godsend after all.

"I can't believe it. I'm at the top of the Hyalite Peak overlooking the entire city of Bozeman. This journey has been unforgettable and like nothing I've ever experienced before. I learned so much about myself and honestly, didn't expect myself to make it to the top — at least not as quickly as I did. Alhamdulilah.

Once again, I'm amazed by His mercy and His power. He is the One who gave me the ability to climb this mountain and get to the top. He allowed me to overcome each obstacle that was thrown my way, out of pure love and mercy. He allowed me to remember Him, even though at times, I was distracted by harsh winds, heavy rain, and physical pain or fatigue. I was able to get through it all — but not just that — I found inner peace because of those struggles. I found solace in knowing that they were blessings in disguise."

Zohra took a few steps and realized that this was it. This was the summit. And it was breathtaking. But what made the view so special wasn't the fact that she made it to the top, or even how gorgeous it looked. What made it special was her patience, determination, persistence, and all the lessons she learned along the way. Within each obstacle hid a beautiful lesson of hope. She knew that if she kept trying and remained patient, she would get to the top, and she did.

CONTENTMENT

Sometimes you have to pause for a moment, take a step back, and appreciate all your blessings — even the ones that you once saw as misfortunes. Surely, we plot and plan, but He is the best of planners, and His plan is always greater.

God wills and causes events to occur at appropriate times, for precise reasons, with flawless wisdom. When God decrees something for His slave, whether it is a celebratory event or a calamity, no one has the power or ability to block or remove it, for there is no power and no strength except with Allah.

Everything in this life is preordained, from your sustenance and *rizq* (provisions); your sickness, health and happiness; and your trials and hardships. So know that whatever God has decreed for you, whether it appears positive or negative; you should not hate, dislike, or show any discomfort towards it.

"No disaster upon the earth or among yourselves except that it is in a register before We bring it into being - indeed that, for Allah, is easy - so that you do not despair over what has eluded you and not exult in pride over what He has given you." - (The Qur'an, 57:22-23)

Ibn Kathir mentioned in his Tafsir, "...whoever suffered an affliction and he knew that it occurred by Allah's judgment and decree, then God guides his heart, and will compensate him for his loss in this life by granting guidance to his heart and certainty in faith. God will replace whatever he lost for Him with the same or what is better. Therefore, he will know that what reached him would not have missed him and what has missed him would not have reached him." - (Volume 10:24-25)

So have *tawakkul* (trust) in Allah's wisdom for the events that unfold in your lives, and accept His decree. He will steer your heart to the tranquility of knowing that whatever you encounter could never have missed you and whatever you lose, could never have reached you.

Know that God will never disappoint a sincere caller. Even when you think he hasn't answered you, He has already planned in your favor. So put your utmost trust in Him and seek His guidance; indeed the Almighty is the best of Planners.

THE CAVE

Half of love lies within the realms of sacrifice. Be it your comfort, your free time, your bad habits; at some point, you need to let go of things for the sake of your most important relationships.

Let's recall the story of *ashab ul-kahf* (the youth in the cave). They chose discomfort over luxury — the cold stone floors of the cave over the warmth of their cots. Their sharp vision helped them distinguish between fleeting agony and perpetual bliss, showing them how much reward lies within surrendering oneself to His pleasure. The youth supplicated to, believed in and feared Allah, and so in return, He granted them the gift of firmness. He strengthened their hearts and increased them in guidance. "… and We made firm their hearts when they stood up and said, 'Our Lord is the Lord of the heavens and the earth. Never will we invoke any deity besides Him. We would have certainly spoken, then, an excessive transgression.'" - (The Qur'an, 18:13-14)

A few verses later, Allah (SWT) says: "And when you forsake them [your people] and what they worship save Allah, then seek for refuge to the cave; your Lord will spread for you of His mercy, and make for you an easy way out of your ordeal." - (The Qur'an, 18:16)

What a beautiful message from the pen of our Lord, perpetrating the beauty found within the depths of struggle. There is ease given by Him when we place our misdirected desires to the side and hang on tightly to His rope.

Yanshur lakum [يَنشُرْ لَكُمْ] translates to, "He will expand for you."

When we give up something for His sake, our intentions and efforts don't go unnoticed. He ensures that He will provide for us a means of relaxation from our decision. Think about it: nature abandoned its usual ways for the youth in the cave. The sun shifted its course, beating its rays away from their faces as it rose and set — unexpected protection. So while the cave you are residing in might feel tight, in reality, it is an opening for His mercy — a spiritual reassurance and physical protection.

CRIES OF ALHAMDULILAH

One of the greatest tricks of the *Shaytan* is how he sways you into thinking that a specific person is bringing you closer to God when no one can actually bring you closer to Him, or take you further away from Him. Your walls need to be strong enough to withhold the pressure you feel when enticed to sin or steer from a good deed.

His words need to be the brick and cement that build your home. Your encounters with each person, as well as situation, need to be greeted with a smile that's rooted from a heart filled with His light. Your heart should be so filled with that Light (and love), placed into you by Him, that the greatest insult from another person doesn't affect you for too long; you know that God is *al-Hafiz*, the One who Protects. You need to fight harder in the *jihad* (fight) against your *nafs* (ego), remembering that it's an endless battle — the real test of life that determines how much of His pleasure you'll find There.

Don't ever rely on or expect another person, even if they're your spouse, to bring you closer to Him. It's all you. You should always work to be the strongest, and for that, you need your fuel. Make repentance as much as possible. Remember Him wherever you go — in your heart, in your mind, and on your tongue. Read the Qur'an. Let it become the cynosure that guides your every action.

You need to abide by His law and stop making excuses for yourself, only to falsify your wrongs into rights.

If someone is helping you sin, regardless of their excuses (or your own in helping yourself sin), you need first to cut off the root of the problem. Now, if you're already in a slump, the only thing that will get you out is something outside of that slump.

It's so clear to see. This is when you know you have to let them go. And of course, the longer you've been playing with the whisperer, the harder it is to do so. You'll want to give yourself reasons to stay, telling yourself that this person has good intentions and a pure heart. Maybe you're right. Perhaps they do have pure intentions. It's important to realize that intentions are easily skewed and manipulated though.

You'll be stubborn about wanting to keep your word, but be smarter than that. Don't ignore your sharp intuition and the universal language of the heart. You'll know when something isn't right for you, and when you come to realize it, revel in that moment of despair and complete desperateness in needing your Lord. This is the blessing of opened eyes and an opened heart; it's the beauty of being granted a criterion from the Almighty. Your heart will cry out *Astaghfirullah* while your body is in a state of *Alhamdulilah* — it's hard to describe. The eyes you shut the truth to were finally opened to that same truth, by the insurmountable mercy of Allah, the Most Loving.

Allah (SWT) tells us, "O you who have believed, if you fear Allah, He will grant you a criterion and will remove from you your misdeeds and forgive you. And God is the possessor of great bounty." - (The Qur'an, 8:29)

So Allah is going to show you how to judge between right and wrong.

There are people in your past who hurt you in a way that's difficult to accept, without a doubt. At some point, you cared for them and naturally wanted to make excuses for them, but there's a limit to everything. Not concerning amount, but in a person's role and relation to you. You became attached to an idea, not a person, without ever acknowledging it. And through that attachment, your focus, purpose, and intentions were distorted. These are the tricks of the *Shaytan*. When you're in that slump, it's easier to dig yourself a deeper hole than to climb out.

His tricks can't beat God's mercy though. No, they can't even come close. It's all about *haqq* (right) and *batil* (wrong). Truth always destroys falsehood. You'll feel the way the mere thought of them makes your insides crumble. You'll feel this sharp, almost tangible pain in your chest, knocking on the walls around your heart, trying to break them down. You'll feel a hollowness where your intense desire to continue working harder used to be, whenever you're reminded of that person. This last point is an important one. We work harder as a means to reach our ends: finding His pleasure in this world and the Next. When you see that your motivation to continue working for His sake is at a decline, it's a sign that you're in a dangerous place.

When the puzzle pieces fall together and reality hits you, you'll be at a loss for every single thing, aside from running to your Lord with the truth in your hand, begging for forgiveness. You paid no heed for so long to what He was giving you clear signs to see. Your arrogance and ignorance killed you. You'll wish you listened sooner. You'll wish you had never put even that minimal amount of hope into reaching a particular place, through the one person who destroyed you. You learned though. Every single person who comes into your life teaches you a lesson.

So you accept the truth and your faults, while forgiving yourself and all those you wrongly associate with those faults. You have to keep moving forward. Use the weight that's on your shoulders to strengthen you. If you fall, stand back up. Train harder and give yourself optimal nourishment for optimal health. And then, make more significant goals. Fulfill your role as His beloved servant, continually observing and reflecting within, digging deeper, fighting against your ego, all while making *du'a* that He accepts your efforts and is pleased with them.

Find consistency, and work hard at achieving that before focusing on reaching your goal. This is a marathon, not a sprint. Signs of change might not be apparent immediately, but over time, God Willing, you'll see the growth.

Always try to be cognizant of your ends and never confuse it with your means. The goal is to live while inculcating the Qur'an and *Sunnah*, and to die in a way that's pleasurable to God.

May He give us all the ability to do so.

ACKNOWLEDGEMENTS

Writing a book and trying to put it together requires a significant amount of patience, encouragement, support, and inspiration. This book wouldn't have been possible without (all of the above) from my husband, Babar, who was with me through all the highs and lows while I was completing this book. He even named it. Thank you, love.

I am forever grateful to my parents, who taught me some of the most valuable life skills: discipline, manners, respect, and love for God. They have always encouraged me to think outside the box and dream big.

To my three older siblings: Bajoo, Adil bhai, and Khalid bhai. I have learned so many great qualities from each of you. Thank you for shaping a huge part of whom I've become.

To everyone at Leaf Publishing House — the editors, designers, and illustrators. You exceeded my expectations in making this dream come to life. Thank you.

Thank you to Husnah Khan, my dear friend who took the time to revise my book, and pushed me to get my words out there whenever I was feeling doubtful.

To Rania Abuisnaineh, my muse in the world of putting together words in a way that creates masterpieces, who has helped keep my love for writing alive and ignited.

To those who questioned my abilities or tried to make me believe that I was incapable, thank you for pushing me to feel otherwise.

To my readers and supporters, I appreciate you. Your love and kindness doesn't go unnoticed — in fact, it has been one of my biggest blessings.

CPSIA information can be obtained
at www.ICGtesting.com
Printed in the USA
BVHW031456240222
630007BV00003B/173

9 781999 955250